Third Party

Corporate

Training

Third Party Corporate Training

Opportunities and Challenges

Facing Small and Medium Sized

Businesses in Alberta

An Avason Consulting Publication

Written By:

Kurt V. Spady, MBA

Third Party Corporate Training – Opportunities and Challenges Facing Small and Medium Sized Business in Alberta

ISBN: 978-0-9936673-0-5

Visit our website at http://www.avasonconsulting.com

Book design by Janelle Spady

Library and Archives Canada has catalogued this edition as follows:

Spady, Kurt V., 1983 –

Third Party Corporate Training – Opportunities and Challenges Facing Small and Medium Sized Businesses in Alberta / By Kurt Spady

Published and distributed by Avason Consulting Corp.
PO BOX 25059
Red Deer, Alberta, Canada T4R 2M2
Telephone - (403) 596-8389
Email – customerservice@avasonconsulting.com

To my wife Janelle,

with whose love and support I have found that anything is possible

Abstract

The purpose of this research and analysis is to investigate opportunities and challenges that face private sector small and medium sized businesses in the province of Alberta, related to employee training by third party corporate training providers. These opportunities and challenges will be tied to organizational goals including but not limited to; employee productivity, management effectiveness, cost effective training, and organizational culture.

The methodology for conducting the required research was to review the literature related to corporate training, and the factors affecting this for both individual employees, and organizations. Relevant market data for small and medium sized enterprises (SME) in Alberta was also reviewed and compared with the research in order to draw conclusions and make recommendations.

An analysis of the literature and relevant data for SMEs in Alberta revealed the following key findings:

- Due to rapidly changing workforce demographics, advances in technology, and an increasingly globalized competitive environment, corporate training remains a main source of developing a skilled workforce in order to maintain a competitive advantage due to these conditions.
- Technological advances continue to lower cost and increase the quality and convenience of employee training options. It also helps SMEs leverage cost savings associated with the economies of scale that can be provided by third party corporate training partners.
- Training initiatives show a positive correlation with employee satisfaction, leading to more productive employees and high quality outputs.

1

- Corporate training also supports foundational behavioral models that show a linkage between training as having positive effects on employee behavior.
- Training opportunities in general are not equally distributed amongst employee groups, with older employees and lower skilled workers receiving fewer opportunities for training.
- Training should be approached by aligning it with organizational as well as individual employee objectives, as this is the key determinate in terms of the degree of the success of training.
- Although any type of return on investment analysis is costly and subjective, it has been shown that with a longitudinal approach to researching this, quantifiable benefits can be shown. The same idea relates to benchmarking corporate training initiatives; because each organization is different in terms of its training goals and objectives, structure, and overall approach, these types of evaluations result in subjective comparisons.
- Corporate training is essentially an investment in human capital for an organization, as well as for employees themselves. Because of this, there are costs and benefits that must be borne by both parties. This also relates to specific versus general training, where the balance of costs and benefits can vary, but in general, firm specific training is more valuable to the organization and general training is more valuable to the employee. This is because general training can be transferred to other positions or organizations.

Failure rates for small and medium sized private sector businesses in Alberta and elsewhere continue to be high, due to reasons often cited that could be improved through employee corporate training. It is recommended that all SMEs in Alberta pursue an organizational goal and development plan, and then engage in a corporate training initiative. This can most cost effectively be accomplished through a third party corporate training provider for the organization to best

2

address challenges and receive the maximum level of benefit that can be realized through an employee corporate training initiative, as detailed in the following sections of this book.

Third Party Corporate Training
Opportunities and Challenges Facing Small and Medium Sized
Businesses in Alberta

Table of Contents

6

1.0 Introduction

The research contained in this book will address management issues facing small and medium sized businesses in Alberta, with respect to the benefits and challenges that surround corporate training of their employees.

The scope of the research will focus on how literature and relevant theories relate to training providers whose primary business operations fall within the North American Industry Classification System #611143– Professional and Management Development Training (Statistics Canada, 2010).

It will specifically be addressed in this report whether or not there appears to be benefits for small and medium sized businesses in Alberta. And also what key elements would be required for successful leveraging of third party corporate training opportunities.

It is hypothesized that corporate training will have benefits for small and medium sized organizations. However, the qualitative aspects of the research to support this broad concept will be the focus of this paper. Secondary data will be utilized to complete this analysis and support the proposed hypothesis.

For the purpose of this research it will be assumed that the definition of small and medium sized businesses will be that of Industry Canada (2012) that defines small and medium sized enterprises (SME's) as being all businesses with fewer than 500 employees.

For the purposes of this book research will not focus on micro-enterprises, which are defined by Industry Canada (2012) as a business having fewer than 5 employees.

2.0 Research Purpose and Research Questions

The purpose of this research is to further explore the benefits and challenges of corporate training, particularly for small and medium sized businesses. These opportunities and challenges will be related to organizational goals including but not limited to employee productivity, management effectiveness, cost effective training, or organizational culture.

The existence of multiple training organizations, indicate that there is presumably a benefit for organizations to pay to train their employees. However, what those benefits are, and what limitations exist in the marketplace that could be served by third party organizations is information that is not readily available, or is not clear.

Relevant literature indicates that continuous training of employees supports a learning culture that enables an organization to be more adaptable and competitive in the current globalized marketplace. However, the opportunities and challenges for this type of training for small and medium sized businesses are not as clearly defined. This is due to the fact that the majority of employee training is done by large corporations, and public organizations.

Research questions to be addressed are:

Primary Research Question:

What are the opportunities and challenges faced by small and medium sized private sector businesses in Alberta to invest in third party corporate training?

Sub-questions:

What economic benefits will be realized by businesses that invest in third party corporate training and why?

What kinds of training options exist for small and medium sized private sector businesses and why?

This research is of value as it will seek to understand the opportunities and challenges faced by small and medium sized private sector businesses in Alberta. This will better allow for these companies, as well as training providers, to better understand the value of third party corporate training for small and medium sized businesses.

The research question will be adequately addressed when a comprehensive overview of opportunities and challenges related to a variety of organizational goals for employee training has been analyzed. This will allow findings of opportunities and challenges to be measured against similar and contrasting organizational goals related to third party corporate training.

3.0 Review of Literature and Related Theory

3.1 Review of Literature

The literature review will explore the benefits and challenges of corporate training for organizations, and in particular, third party corporate training for small and medium sized private sector businesses. The review will also look at how corporate training is generally approached in terms of where it is provided, when it is provided, and who provides the training.

Literature will be reviewed from the last 10 years, as well as some foundational works that have been core concepts over time. This timeline will reflect the significant changes in technology and the global economy that have occurred, which have subsequently affected the corporate training industry.

3.2 Benefits of Corporate Training

The general consensus of most research is that there are benefits of corporate training for organizations, but that in terms of a return on investment, there is no way to quantify these benefits to an organization's bottom line (Newton & Doonga, 2007, Melnik, 2008, Kirkpatrick, 2010, Bernier & Cousineau, 2010, Hardman & Robertson, 2012). This is also supported by the fact that appropriate data for analyzing on the job training is lacking (Salas-Valesco, 2006, Bernier & Cousineau, 2010). Matalonga and Feliu (2010) suggest that there is no consensus for whether or not an ROI calculation for employee training must be carried out. This is the issue that will be addressed by the research; if it is not feasible to calculate an ROI, why should an organization invest in the training of its employees? Can it be shown what the qualitative and quantitative benefits are and if it cannot be shown that they lead directly to the bottom line, how can it be shown

10

that corporate training will indirectly lead to an increase in the organizations profits? This information will address the question of whether corporate training is a worthwhile investment decision.

Rivera's (2009) longitudinal study of employee training confirms that investments in training were not significantly linked to financial outcomes. However, Rivera (2009) also states that while associations were not clearly demonstrated, that neither was the absence of such associations. The benefits of training appear to be multi-dimensional (Rivera, 2009).

Hansson (2008) states that employer sponsored training is the most important source of further education and training for an individual after they enter the labor market. Hansson (2008) also states that employer financed training reduces the probability of an individual, once trained, to leave the organization.

However Hansson, (2008) also concludes that employer sponsored training benefits are higher for the organization, should the employee be retained, and higher for the employee should they leave the organization for another position elsewhere.

3.3 The Need for Corporate Training

There is also a general consensus in a variety of research that suggests the need for continuous training of employees is needed due to the shift towards a knowledge economy, rapidly changing technology, globalization, and an increasingly diverse workforce (Meyer & Marsick, 2003, ASHE, 2002, Newton & Doonga, 2007). However, Newton and Doonga (2007) also point out that it is important not to overemphasize technological change as impacting training delivery itself, as the majority of learning still occurs in the classroom (Hardman & Robertson, 2012). This leads to the hypothesis that all organizations face these challenges. However, what is the degree of variance for organizations in Alberta, in different industries, and for employee

11

positions within those industries? At what degree of significance are these factors impacting the need for corporate training?

Training is also not equally distributed amongst employees. Hansson (2008) states that older, lower skilled workers, and to a certain extent female workers, receive less training than other groups of employees. However, Hanson (2008) also states that there is no evidence to suggest that training varies due to factors such as gender (for the most part), educational or skill level. This suggests that unequal distribution arises not because of a difference in the return on investment, but more likely because of the inequalities related to the distribution of investment.

Plante (2005) states that access and barrier issues to training in the workplace are more often rooted in employer factors than they are in employee factors.

Craig (1996) addresses the need for training by attempting to answer the question, "why train now?" by answering the following:

1.   Realigning the workforce after a merger, globalization, new initiative
2.   Training newly appointed leaders
3.   Preparing future leaders

3.4 Evaluating Training Initiatives

Evaluating corporate training is another area where very similar themes appear in the research. It is generally understood that benefits and return on investment of corporate training is difficult to ascertain. The work of Donald Kirkpatrick is cited in numerous research papers as a common and appropriate method for evaluating training (ASHE, 2002, Newton & Doonga, 2007, Kirkpatrick, 2010). However, this work was from his publication Techniques for Evaluating Training Programs and was published in 1959. Due to the reasons cited for companies to continually engage in corporate training, which are relatively new, perhaps a more contemporary model for evaluation of training would be appropriate. Also, in terms of the four levels of evaluation, (1 – reaction 2 – learning 3 – transfer to the job 4 – organizational effects) levels 3 and 4 are typically too cumbersome to complete. Also some evaluations stop at levels 1 and 2, often simply asking the participants if they liked the training (ASHE, 2002, Hardman & Robertson, 2012). Motorola is cited in as spending over a million dollars to assess the return on investment of its training program (ASHE, 2002).

Input measures can also be used to evaluate training value from a quality perspective, under the assumption that more input equals better outcomes. These input measures could include metrics such as hours of training per employee per year, training expenditures as a percentage of payrolls, or ratio of employers to trainers (ASHE, 2002). The issue with this is that this is not always the case and can be a subjective analysis of training benefits. More money spent does not always mean better quality outcomes. The literature indicates that at best, evaluation methods for training initiatives are subjective, and at worst, misleading.

Bernier and Cousineau (2010) conducted a study that was able to identify that there are in fact quantifiable benefits and a financial return on investment for corporate training. This occurs if you consider taking into account a longitudinal approach to employees receiving benefits from training. However, this analysis is subjective and the authors acknowledge that indirect benefits may likely also occur. Matalonga and Feliu (2010) also support this by stating that any training ROI must be accompanied by a reference to time so that it can be compared to other investments. A Josh Bersin study, as cited in Kirkpatrick (2010), indicated the percentage of learning and value occurring before, during, and after training, suggesting it is quite difficult to access the true qualitative and quantitative benefits for a company based only on the training event itself. Dobrovolny (2006) supports this by stating that participants in his study benefitted by having access to training materials after the training, to refresh their memory and answer questions. Kirkpatrick (2010) also states that it is a trap trainers get into when they suggest that training by itself leads to bottom line results, and suggests this is impossible without a supportive

13

work environment and managers to reinforce learning and hold employees accountable for training deliverables. It appears clear that an approach to training that exceeds simply conducting the training event leads to what would be considered the ROI to an organization. It is clear from the research that events leading up to, during, and after a training event in conjunction with work environment and management support is what leads to the benefits of training. These benefits also appear to exist in a variety of capacities.

Benchmarking is cited as another approach to defining and evaluating the benefits of corporate training in terms of a return on investment (ASHE, 2002). However, this may simply be a relationship of association amongst the data, rather than causation. Also, this may differ widely for various occupations and industries. This is because the only way to benchmark for productivity evaluation is to find similar organizations and training programs (ASHE, 2002), which would likely be very difficult. In the private sector, an employee's position within the organization is an important determinant of on the job training (Kyndt, Dochy, Onghena, Baert, 2013). This again would be difficult to benchmark against depending on the variance of duties between the same types of positions at different organizations.

3.5 Training as a Shared Investment

The concept of mutual benefit is also explored in various papers including ASHE (2002), Salas-Valesco (2006), Chan, Miller & Monroe (2009), Kirkpatrick (2010), and Bernier & Cousineau (2010). In general, the training opportunities must be both beneficial for the employer and the employee for both parties to engage in corporate training opportunities. By sharing in the investment, each party is less likely to terminate the relationship (Salas-Valesco, 2006). However, this research does not differentiate between compulsory training, such as health and safety training, and discretional training such as conflict resolution. It could be inferred that the term "mutually beneficial training" could include a scope much broader than what was addressed

14

in these papers, in terms of training as a shared investment to be made by both parties.

Companies are reluctant to invest in employee training for the fact that employees may leave the organization (Bernier & Cousineau, 2010). However, it has been shown that in fact providing employees with training can lead to increased loyalty and retention (ASHE, 2002, Bernier & Cousineau, 2010, Kyndt et al, 2012). This appears to be an issue of competing priorities. Research indicates that there are barriers experienced by organizations providing employee training that must be overcome before it can take place, and the organization can receive benefit from it.

As stated by Ballot, Fakhfakh and Taymaz (2006) the organization appears to experience the largest return on a training investment that it makes, as opposed to the employee. This would hold true as long as the employee was retained by the organization that trained them, otherwise the return on training would go to the employee, leaving the organization for another position that utilizes their training.

3.6 Employee Groups Participating in Corporate Training

Kyndt, Dochy, Onghena, and Baert (2013) conducted a study that showed the likeliness of various groups of employees to receive training. For example that groups of employees receiving low compensation in jobs that require little education, received less training opportunities than their highly compensated, higher educated counterparts. This is also supported by Hardman and Robertson (2013). Other studies support this showing that in general, people that are more educated going into the workforce are more likely to receive training opportunities (for example Doctors and Lawyers would receive the most) (Salas-Valesco, 2006). However, there is also the concept that if formal education and occupational training are substitutive, then over-educated workers will invest less in training, and undereducated workers will invest more in occupational training (Kyndt et al, 2013).

15

The issue appears to be who is provided the opportunity for this training, why, and who is paying for it. It could be inferred that this will be different depending on industry and qualifications required for various positions within each industry.

It appears that large organizations, as well as public organizations, are the majority of users of corporate training (ASHE, 2002, Salas-Valesco, 2006), Kyndt et al, 2013). Many of these organizations develop their own training in-house. This situation appears to be an issue of limited resources, limited economies of scale, and competing priorities for small and medium sized enterprises (Kyndt et al, 2013). Ashton and Green (1996) as cited in Kyndt et al (2013) indicates that large firms generally retain the employees they train, while small and medium sized businesses do not have the same capacity for promotions and salary increases as a result of the training. There are conflicting issues in the research showing that although training is beneficial, certain organizations are not able to facilitate training that would result in benefits for the organization. This appears to be especially dependent on the organizations size and level of resources. There is also contrasting data presented by Miller (2012), who shows that on a per employee basis, SME's spend more money than larger organizations.

3.7 Keys to Successful Corporate Training

One of the keys to successful corporate training is cited as being the ability to align training with an organization's mission and goals (Meyer & Marsick, 2003, ASHE, 2002). The issue with this approach may be that although the organization's mission and goals say one thing, actual operations and operational issues may be different. This is an issue that may be a missed opportunity for organizations that are unaware of this issue, and which could also be addressed through employee training at the organizational level. Another key to successful training cited in several studies is support from line managers and the CEO of the organization (ASHE, 2002).

Training programs are increasingly successful if they are incorporated with a practical application component (Meyer & Marsick, 2003, Cekada, 2011). This poses an interesting situation for training providers that may not be able to facilitate this. As an example, training providers who are here one day and gone the next provides them with no opportunity to see how the training is impacting the organization. Or for example, a Massive Online Open Course (MOOC) that is very far removed from an organization and is unable to truly be a strategic partner. Due to the fact that meaningful training should include active learning and debriefings, this would not be able to occur under a MOOC delivery model. Other open source courseware training options would have this limitation as well.

3.8 Online Corporate Training

Online learning is a large focus of contemporary employee training. Several studies cite numerous options for providing online training including self-directed, trainer facilitated, and blended learning (ASHE, 2002, Newton & Doonga, 2007). It should also be noted that the majority of training continues to be classroom based instruction (ASHE, 2002). E-learning can also be costly, have weak reporting systems, and depending on the delivery can create lower participation rates (Newton & Doonga, 2007, Hardman & Robertson, 2012). However, there are also a variety of benefits such as anytime anywhere training that leverages economies of scale (Newton & Doonga, Hardman & Robertson, 2012). In general, there are several benefits and costs of online learning which may or may not be appropriate depending on the organization. The flexibility of online learning also poses a risk of negatively impacting an employee's work life balance (Joo, Lyn & Kim, 2012).

It should also be noted that, in terms of individual learning, that there is no significant difference between online learning and in-classroom learning (ASHE, 2002). Although Dobrovolny (2006) cites Dalton et. al, as conducting a study indicating that students master self-paced technology instruction in less time than with group instruction. Adults above college age were not included in the study. Dobrovolny (2006) states that as long as training is facilitated in a way that involves blended learning and a comprehensive approach in terms of learning methods, that that is the key for successful learning objectives of corporate training. There is also no differentiation by gender, although women overall take less training (Kyndt et al, 2013)

Rossett (2002) states that e-learning has been gaining credibility over the years and has been bringing visibility and credibility to the training industry for the following reasons:

1. Accepted recognition that human capital is the cornerstone of the new economy and central to the value of a company and its ability to innovate.
2. The increasing influx of capital, investment partners, and external players in the e-learning marketplace.
3. The reach, consistency, and growing sophistication of the internet as a vehicle for training.
4. The realization that education and learning methods are based on past models and practices.

Rossett (2002) also states that e-learning provides the following learner benefits:

1. Instant access
2. Universal access
3. Virtual collaboration
4. Learner control

3.9 Human Capital Theory

Human capital theory can be used to show conceptually why corporate training is beneficial to organizations. It can also be used to show that in a perfectly competitive labor market, firms would have no incentive to invest in the general training of their workforce (Salas-Valesco,

2006, Bernier & Cousineau, 2010). This is supported by Kyndt et al (2013), in that specific training allows the firm to capture more accurately the benefits of the training, which is more difficult to do for general training. Also, Thurow (1975) as cited in Kyndt et al (2013), predicted that employers would want to hire over educated workers, as they would not have to train them themselves. So employees without this education would benefit from corporate training.

Becker (1964) wrote a foundational work describing Human Capital Theory. It looks at activities that influence both future and monetary psychic income by increasing the resources in people, or investments in human capital. These investments could include formal schooling, on the job training, medical care, migration, and searching for information on prices and incomes (Becker, 1964).

Becker (1964) cites that few if any counties have been able to sustain economic development without substantial investment in the development of their labor force. This finding could be related to the importance of companies to do the same.

Workers will increase their productivity by learning new skills and perfecting old ones while on the job and future productivity can be improved only at a cost, otherwise there would be an unlimited demand for training (Becker, 1964).

Most training will presumably increase the future marginal productivity of workers in the firms providing it. However, general training increases the potential for that marginal product being realized at other firms as well (Becker, 1964). This is related to the idea that general corporate training investment benefits can only be realized by a business should the trained employee remain with that organization.

Becker (1964) describes the analogy of a trained employee to a patent that would eventually provide external benefits to other companies once it expired. This, Becker (1964) states, would be similar to a trained employee leaving an organization for another. The difference

19

in the analogies is that the firm has the option to increase wages for the employee to stop them from looking elsewhere for employment. This would not be the case in the patent situation.

The productivity of employees depends on their ability, the amount invested in them both on and off the job, their motivation, and the intensity of their work (Becker, 1964). This would also vary by type of job, type of investment, type of training, and the fact that people of the world differ enormously in productivity. These differences are largely related to environmental factors and these in turn are related to accumulation of knowledge and the maintenance of health (Becker, 1964).

Bassi and McMurrer (2007) suggest a framework for analyzing an organizations human capital. They suggest this, as most traditional metrics such as total training hours provided, do not accurately predict organizational performance. They suggest looking at the categories of Leadership Practices, Employee Engagement, Knowledge Accessibility, Workforce Optimization, and Learning Capacity. Each of these categories could be directly or indirectly linked to an organizations training initiative.

3.10 Specific versus General Training

Specific versus general training is distinguished by showing that general training is beneficial to employees as it is valuable anywhere they go (Salas-Valesco, 2006). This is in contrast to specific training, which is only beneficial to an employee while they are working for that particular company (Salas-Valesco, 2006). Mandatory versus discretional training also impacts the degree of success that corporate training has for the organization and its employees (Salas-Valesco, 2006).

Hansson (2008) indicates that most training that is employer sponsored is general in nature. Estimates suggest that general training constitutes

20

somewhere between 60-90% of all employer sponsored training (Hansson, 2008).

Bird (1973) states that, in a survey conducted, employee relations (general training) was by far the most requested type of training (40%) by company owners and executives. This is reinforced today by Miller (2012) who states that one of the top three categories of training requested is managerial and supervisory training.

3.11 Training and Employee Satisfaction

Batool (2012) links employee training to decreases in employee turnover levels and increased satisfaction, and views this trend as a source of competitive advantage.

McEvoy and Buller (1990) suggest some criteria to consider when evaluating training as related to employee and employer satisfaction with training outcomes:

1. Work vs Perk – is the training attempting to improve work performance or is it a prerequisite for job performance that has already been shown to be successful.
2. Substance vs Symbol – Is the training part of the basic underlying culture of the organization, or is it the organization expressing a rite of passage, enhancement, or renewal.
3. External vs Internal Training – For example to instill company pride, or follow external best practices.
4. Behaviors vs Outcomes – Is the training designed to change behavior (increase self-awareness / insight) or to learn or improve skills to increase work outcomes (increased output).
5. Self Ratings vs Other Ratings – For example evaluating whether the employees liked the training, or was the

training goal to challenge existing perceptions within the organization.

Other issues discussed by McEvoy and Buller (1990) related to satisfaction with the training experience include things like:

1. Hidden agendas of training sessions, for example is it a perk, or done to improve work outcomes, or to make a hiring decision.
2. Real or perceived significance of the training, from both an employee and employer perspective.
3. Emphasis on accountability, versus ability to demonstrate performance results to verify training outcome goals (for example intangible goals that are difficult to measure.)

3.12 How Corporate Training Should Be Designed

In terms of structuring training, Gange and Briggs (1979) state that although learners are often assembled in groups, training designs must be aimed at the learning of the individual.

Friedenberg (1965) and Barth (1972) as cited in Gagne and Briggs (1979) suggest that education would be best if designed simply as a nurturing environment to allow people to grow in their own ways.

Learning outcomes of training are multidimensional and can include intellectual skills, cognitive strategies, verbal information, motor skills, and attitudes; with each of these categories being able to be improved through learning (Gagne & Briggs, 1979).

Gagne and Briggs (1979) also state that special means of instruction are not required for learning to occur; it is simply required that the individual learner possesses the skills for interpretation of the information through a variety of media. This relates to the concepts underlying online training and its ability to grow as a medium of learning facilitation.

Effects of necessary instructional events on the individual learner decreases as the instructional group increases in size (Gagne & Briggs, 1979). This will be an important consideration for SMEs wanting to conduct training sessions, and how they will structure the learning environment.

Gagne and Briggs (1979) suggest that a training course could be evaluated by asking the following questions:

1. To what extent have the stated goals or objectives of instruction been met?
2. In what ways and to what degree are those results better or worse than what was in place before the training?
3. What additional, and possibly unanticipated, effects or outcomes has the training had, and to what extent is this better or worse than what was in place before training occurred?

Scriven, as cited in Gagne and Briggs (1979), suggests the goal free evaluation as a method to evaluate a training initiative. This means to assess the effects, and the worth of the effects, whatever those might be. This will be an important consideration for SMEs with regards to how they will evaluate the value of their training initiatives. Stufflebeam (1971) suggests that goal free evaluation is a good additional supplement to goal based evaluation.

Scriven, as cited in Gagne and Briggs (1979), also suggests evaluating a product as follows:

1. Need – establishing that the product will contribute to the health or survival of an organization
2. Market – determine that there is a plan for getting and using the product.
3. Performance in field trials – evidence of performance of the product in similar conditions

4. Consumer performance – the appropriateness with which the product is addressed (to employees) and the likeliness that it will be used by these consumers
5. Performance comparisons
6. Performance long term
7. Performance side effects
8. Performance process
9. Performance causation
10. Statistical significance – quantitative indicator of effect
11. Educational significance
12. Costs and cost effectiveness
13. Extended support

3.13 Related Theories to Support Employee Training

Craig (1996) states that there are four main reasons why organizations have moved towards a culture of learning:

1. Competitive Environment
2. Rate of change – technology
3. Personal Fulfillment
4. Demand for creativity and innovation

As a result of these factors, things like diversity training and training for global operations have become important parts of organizational training initiatives (Craig, 1996).

Craig (1996) cites several theories related to employee training and development which are as follows:

- Douglas McGregor – Theory X and Y. Theory X suggests an inherent dislike for work and that employees will seek to do the minimum amount of work possible. Theory Y suggests that people will naturally seek out and accept responsibility, that work is a natural part of the human condition.

24

- Abraham H. Maslow – Maslow's hierarchy of needs states that needs at the bottom of the pyramid must be fulfilled before needs at the top can be realized. For example, a person will need to fulfill the need of food and shelter before they will seek safety needs and so on. Craig (1996) also states that for people reaching levels of self-actualization, that this is a rare occurrence. Maslow's hierarchy of needs consists of the following (number one is the top of the pyramid):

  1. Self-Actualization
  2. Esteem Needs
  3. Belonging and Love Needs
  4. Safety Needs
  5. Physiological Needs

- Frederick Herzberg – Two Factor Theory – States that the opposite of satisfaction is not dissatisfaction, but no satisfaction. These factors come in the form of Satisfiers and Dissatisfiers, which are also called growth needs (satisfiers) and hygiene factors (dissatisfiers).

- Myers Briggs – Is a personality type indicator that categorizes people into a certain category of personality type.

- Carl Jung – Jungian psychology is also the basis for various personality type indicators based on the work of Carl Jung which, similar to Myers Briggs, categorizes people into a certain category of personality type.

- Donald Kirkpatrick Model – This model is used for the evaluation of training initiatives:

Step 1 – Reaction – how well did they like it

25

Step 2 – Learning – what was learned, what attitudes were changed

Step 3 – Behavior – What changes in behavior resulted

Step 4 – Results – what were the tangible results of the program in terms of reduced cost, improved quantity, improved quality etc.

Craig (1996) discusses three primary benchmarking types – process, performance and strategic. Utilizing benchmarking may be difficult for a SME because they would need to find other companies in exactly the same situations in order to benchmark against them.

Craig (1996) also discusses the stages of growth and development of organizations, listed as:

1. Formative period – new business getting started and procedures are experimental
2. Rapid-growth period – new business begins to grow exponentially
3. Mature Period – established business
4. Declining Period – market becoming saturated

3.14 Training for Small and Medium Sized Businesses

Cohn (1998) suggests that SME's are not able to invest in corporate training because of factors such as restrictions on time, space, money, and staff. Cohn (1998) also states that when corporate training does happen, it is often done in an unstructured manner or on a voluntary basis.

In the United States, of the 6.3 million organizations that would be classified as small or medium sized business, 6 million of those have fewer than 50 employees (Cohn, 1998). Crist, Presley and Zenger (1992) state that 99% of organizations in the United States have fewer than 500 employees and would be considered small or medium sized enterprises. This is true in Canada as well, where most employees work for employers that are SME organizations.

SME's can leverage technology to facilitate collaboration and partner with other organizations, which allows them to realize economies of scale and to have additional options for training (Cohn, 1998). The issue that will have to be addressed by these organizations is who to collaborate with, and who will pay for what expenses related to training initiatives.

Past challenges in terms of the ability of SMEs to invest in training exist today as they did in the past. Bird (1973) indicates that one of the challenges for smaller organizations is that they cannot afford to hire their own highly specialized training staff. This issue exists today in that not only are training staff non-existent in most SMEs, but Human Resources departments who might be better suited to facilitate this training likely do not exist as well.

Kelly (1984) also cites that in 1984 fifty percent of businesses formed will fail within a year primarily because of poor management. Kelly (1984) goes on to state that poor management is often a result of SMEs not having the resources to invest in the training and development that might help to mitigate the risks associated with rapid failure of the business. Statistics Canada (2000) cites that in Canada throughout the provinces, the first year survival rate is rather high ranging from 63-67% for Atlantic Provinces, to a high of 80% in Ontario. The survival rate for new businesses in Alberta is 76% (Statistics Canada, 2000) for the first year. By 5 years, only 37% of new businesses will have survived (Statistics Canada, 2000).

A first consideration for many SMEs, due to a lack of resources, is the cost of training to the organization (Kelly, 1984). Possibly a better approach for SMEs would be to look at what is the cost of not investing in employee training and development. This, as cited by Kelly (1984),

27

would be rapid failure of the business due to a lack of effective management.

Crist, Presley and Zenger (1992) echo Kelly in that few SMEs are providing employee training because they cannot afford to purchase or develop the training by themselves.

Crist et al. (1992) suggest partnerships for SMEs, partnering with training organizations and other SMEs to create a flexible training program that is cost effective. They suggest this by having organizations look at the following:

1. Will the training create a competitive advantage for the business without enduring unreasonable costs?
2. Can the training provider provide the full spectrum of training needs?
3. Will support be available?

Harris (2005) suggests that many challenges that are faced by SMEs can be overcome by leveraging new technologies and engaging in an e-learning or online learning initiative.

Harris (2005) also suggests another challenge for SMEs in terms of corporate training related to current or potential employees. The challenge is that small organizations may find difficulty in determining if individuals have the right skills for their organization, strategies for growth, and how this relates to screening applicants for new or existing positions.

Miller (2012) cites the American Society of Training and Development industry report, which states that in 2011, organizations in the United States spent $156.2 billion on employee learning. Of this amount, 56% was spent internally and the remainder was split between tuition reimbursement (14%) and external services (30%).

In Canada, Plante (2005) states that in 1999-2000, combined public and private expenditures on education totaled $68.6 billion, of which 86%

accounted for public expenditures. This would leave $9.6 billion being spent by organizations internally and on private external services.

In the United States the average per employee expenditure was $1,182 in 2011, down from $1,228 in 2010 ($1,267 adjusted for inflation) (Miller, 2012). Company size is a key determinant of this figure. The report states that smaller companies tend to spend more per employee on training than larger organizations (Miller, 2012). In 2011 SMEs spent on average $1,605 per employee as compared to $1,102 for organizations with more than 500 employees (Miller, 2012). Organizations with more than 10,000 employees spent $805 (Miller, 2012). This could presumably be the result of corresponding economies of scale realized by larger organizations. Miller (2012) states that the cost per learning hour utilized in an SME is $126 compared to $82 for an organization with 500 or more employees, and $51 for organizations with 10,000 or more employees.

3.15 Corporate Training in Canada

Plante (2005) states in her Statistics Canada report on private, for profit education services, that intellectual capital is displacing natural resources as a primary determinant of economic and competitive strength for Canadian businesses. Due to declining fertility, an aging workforce, and massive retirements there is a risk in Canada of a shortage of highly skilled labor (Plante, 2005). Plante (2005) states that private, third party corporate training companies will be key players in meeting Canada's emerging labor market needs.

There are four components of the private, for profit corporate training industry including:

1. Organizations that specialize in education and training programs, their products and services, and conducting training need assessments.

2. Businesses in other sectors (such as accounting, management consulting, or telecommunications) that provide education and training services as a supplement to their main product line or on a standalone basis.
3. Private schools and training institutes.
4. Private, for profit activities of public educational institutions (such as a community college extension services department).

Statistics Canada, as cited in Plante (2005), indicates that 55.7% of firms provide training to their employees in response to a technological change.

Of the 2 million businesses included in Statistics Canada's Business Register (organizations with at least $30,000 in revenue and are incorporated), 20,000, or slightly less than 1% are included in the category of private, for profit third party corporate training. (Plante, 2005).

The Workplace and Employee Survey, as cited in Plante (2005), shows that Ontario has the highest percentage of organizations that offer training (58%). This is followed by British Columbia, Alberta, Saskatchewan and Manitoba (57%), Quebec (49%), and the Atlantic Provinces (41%), having the fewest organizations that supply employee training.

The Adult Education and Training Survey from 2002, as cited by Plante (2005), shows that as firms increase in size, so do the percentage of employees that engage in training. More specifically firms with less than 20 employees having an 18.5% participation rate, 100 – 500 employees with a 32.1% participation rate, and over 500 employee organizations having a 37.2% participations rate (Plane, 2005).

The Adult Education and Training Survey, as cited by Plante (2005), also supports other literature in this book. For example the report shows that all public organizations have a higher rate of third party

30

corporate training participation than private for profit businesses. An example would be Healthcare at 35%, Educational Services 42.6%, Retail 17.3%, and Food Service 11.7% (Plante, 2005).

Plante (2005) suggests that due to the diversity of the Education Services sector in Canada that the first step is to prioritize the information needs of the parties involved, such as:

1. The economic aspects of the organizations sector such as mergers, acquisitions, and the influx of multinational corporations into the Canadian marketplace.
2. Employment levels, earnings, and job stability.
3. Quality of educational services provided by for profit firms, and outcomes for learners including teaching standards, skill enhancements from participation, etc.

3.16 Summary

Employers should train workers because it is a mechanism to increase output per employee and is often part of a recruitment package (Kyndt et al, 2013). However, Hardman and Robertson (2012), as well as Cekada (2011), state that resources spent on training and development of employees can be wasted if the training is not first aligned with organizational goals and objectives. Kyndt et al. (2013) further states that training should be approached as a shared investment between employee and employer. Kyndt et al. (2013) also suggests that training be facilitated with a blended learning approach, be reinforced by management, and that employees should be held to account to utilize training to solve organizational issues. The issue at hand is that the literature fails to differentiate between large organizations and SMEs, and those businesses with potentially different needs and competitive environments.

31

4.0 Research Design and Data Collection

The research design for this book is that of a conceptual research paper, to support or not support the research question and sub questions. The design will be content analysis of existing literature, exploring the challenges and opportunities for corporate training for small and medium sized businesses to identify any patterns, themes, or biases in existing research.

This research design will include publically available secondary data collected from industry reports.

4.1 Components of the Conceptual Research

The approach to this research is conceptual in nature, and involves the use of secondary sources of data. The essence of this conceptual component will be asking questions such as:

- What training opportunities are currently available to SMEs in Alberta?
- What barriers or challenges exist to offer training for SME employees?
- What third party corporate training opportunities could be provided to small and medium sized private sector businesses in Alberta and what are the key elements required to increases the chances of success of this training?

These questions will be answered by reviewing secondary data sources where these questions have been asked. These sources include surveys cited in database research papers, as well as the American Society for Training and Development (ASTD) survey data.

Secondary sources of data include databases including the following sources:

- Pro-quest
- Academic Search Complete
- Statistics Canada
- Industry Canada

As part of a systematic and comprehensive literature search, search terms were:

- Benefits of Corporate training
- Challenges of Corporate Training
- Costs of Corporate Training
- Impacts of Corporate Training

As much of the research is conceptual in nature, the timeframe the research will cover will be any research that has been conducted on these topics within the last 10 years, as well as some foundational works that have become core concepts over time.

5.0 Results

The results of the research can be summarized as follows under the following categories:

5.1 Benefits of Corporate Training

The literature is conclusive in that for an organization to determine any type of a return on the investment in third party corporate training, that this is a difficult task. The research is also conclusive in that attempts to do such evaluations in the past have proven time consuming, costly, and largely subjective.

Several sources cite that the degree to which an organization benefits from training is determined by how well training is aligned with organizational goals. This would presumably indicate that an organization would be required to have well defined organizational goals before it engaged in a third party training investment in order to gain the maximum benefits.

The literature is also in agreement that education and training of workers, if it is aligned with individual and organization goals, will produce a benefit over the long term. The contrast to this idea is that the benefit will either lie largely with the organization if the employee stays, or go with the employee should they leave the organization. In either case it could be argued that overall, third party corporate training for private sector businesses in Alberta would produce a benefit to society, whether economic or otherwise.

The limitation to this idea of the benefits of third party corporate training are as indicated, that if an organization or individual does not have well defined goals for which training can align, it would likely not create a benefit for the organization or individual involved in the training.

34

5.2 The Need for Corporate Training

The literature is in consensus that the need for employee training arises due to the realities of a rapidly changing globalized and technologically advanced environment, and the shift towards a knowledge economy. Training is often cited as a way to mitigate the risks that comes with these factors and as a way to train and realign a workforce.

There are two contrasting issues with this idea. One being that it is highly unlikely that all SMEs, even in a defined geographical location such as Alberta, would all face the same degree of risk and change. It would likely be highly dependent on a variety of factors including size of business, industry, and the employees themselves, in terms of, to what degree do external environmental factors need to be mitigated through employee training.

This leads to the second issue, where the literature states that training is not equally distributed amongst employee groups, and that lower skilled workers tend to receive less training. This also relates to a variety of factors that could affect the degree of need for corporate training, that many people may likely be employed in industries that are less affected by the factors listed above. Factors such as the shift towards a knowledge and service producing economy would likely not affect every business and individual to the same degree. There will likely always be industries or people that will not largely be affected by these factors to a large degree or would not need to have risks mitigated to the same degree.

To summarize the results in the literature around SME third party corporate training investment, it is the employer, not the employee whose factors will drive success. SMEs, in whichever industry they are in, will needs to align their goals and objectives to their training needs to have success in the marketplace.

5.3 Evaluating Training Initiatives

The consistent result that appears in the literature is that corporate training is difficult to evaluate. Several models have been proposed and several levels of evaluation are considered. These range from financial, employee satisfaction, behavior change, output change, input measures (such as dollar spent per employee), and also include various forms of benchmarking.

Studies show consistently that when taking a longitudinal approach to the data, that you can produce quantifiable benefits from training. However, it is acknowledged that there will always be a degree of subjectivity to the results. This is due to the highly likely possibility that indirect factors lead to outcomes that have nothing to do with a training initiative.

In summary, for an SME to expect that it could achieve an objective evaluation of a training initiative is not a feasible option or consideration.

5.4 Training as a Shared Investment

The results of the research indicate that training is a shared investment in terms of costs and benefits that extends beyond the financial. Each party is contributing time, energy, and financial resources, as well as opportunity costs to engage in a training initiative. This creates a situation where both parties now have a stake in any employee training that occurs.

As with any investment there are risks and rewards and both parties risk investing their resources and getting no benefits. The risk to the employee is that they invest in training and get no reward (whether that is financial, self-fulfillment, a promotion etc.). For the employer, the same risk applies in terms of investing in training and the employee

36

does not create additional or increased marginal value for the organization.

Another consideration is the relationship between the employee and the employer. If the employee feels they can get more value from their investment (training) by utilizing it at another organization, they will leave and the employer will lose the benefits they would have received had the employee stayed. For the employer, if they feel their resources are better utilized outside of employee training and development, they will utilize resources in those areas and the employee will not benefit from the training (promotion, self-fulfillment, etc.).

However, studies have indicated that for an employer to forgo employee training, the risk increases that an employee will leave for an organization that will provide this. In this case the employer will lose the investment of all informal training that has occurred (experience, on the job training, knowledge of company operations, etc.).

5.5 Employee Groups Participating in Corporate Training

Two key issues appear in the literature related to various employee groups participating in employee training.

The first is that it appears that employees receiving lower wages in jobs that require a lower level of professional qualifications or formal education receive fewer opportunities for training. Conversely, higher educated and compensated individuals receive more training opportunities.

The second issue is the idea of formal education and corporate training being substitutes. If this is the case, more highly educated workers will invest less in training and employees with lower levels of education will invest more.

The results of the research on human capital would indicate that an SME in an industry that employs individuals with a lower level of

37

education may benefit as these employees may seek to invest in training on their own. However, this situation may also result in the employee leaving the organization if the company cannot provide the employee with an adequate return on their investment. Similarly, an organization with individuals that have a higher level of education may have issues getting their employees to invest in certain types of training, as the employees may see no further benefit.

In terms of different industries, it is also clear that organizations of 500 or more employees, and public organizations, train the most employees. This is related to factors such as resources, economies of scale, number of competing priorities for resources, and these factors would apply to SMEs as well.

5.6 Keys to Successful Corporate Training

The literature outlines factors that should be taken into consideration for organizations to successfully engage in a corporate training initiative.

The first is that success of any training initiative depends on the degree to which it is aligned with the organization's mission and goals.

Support of training from managers, the organization's ownership and senior executive is also cited as a key component of success.

In terms of the structure of the training, training is more likely to be successful if it contains a practical application component that can be utilized by employees to apply learning to the organizational environment.

All of these ideas point to the conclusion that all factors need to be integrated, complete, and in alignment with one another. For example, before senior leaders in the organization can support a training initiative they need to support organizational goals and objectives, which they need to have in order to align with training initiatives.

5.7 Online Corporate Training

Technological change has brought advancement to corporate training that allows for facilitation of training through the internet. This idea has emerged in the research literature over the past ten years. Online training has new cost structures, economies of scale, and new methods of delivering content. These factors address many of the issues that face SMEs with regards to their ability to access training options.

Classroom based training still dominates the third party corporate training landscape, but advances in technology will likely lead to further developments and growth in the online learning option.

Each factor of online learning is addressed in the literature in terms of the costs and benefits of various components. In summary, organizations must make decisions around what level of technological integration of employee training is needed. They must also investigate direct and indirect costs of these initiatives, as there are many.

The summary of the literature indicates that there is no difference in learning outcomes from either online or classroom based training. Although costs and benefits are different, it is catering to learner need which is the key to a successful training initiative. Also, as cited in numerous sources, alignment of training with online initiatives as well as organizational goals and objectives, is a key determinate to the degree in which benefits can be realized from an online facilitation model.

5.8 Human Capital Theory

Human Capital Theory is a foundational theory whose original work is cited in much of the literature surrounding employee training. The theory addresses the idea of employees as a function of the labor market and the degree to which investments in them produces marginal benefits.

The theory states employee training is an investment in human capital, and cites that few if any countries in the world have experienced economic development without this type of investment in their human capital. The theory also states that this increased productivity can only be had at a cost, and the benefits increase only as there is a marginal benefit compared to the cost. This explains why there is not an unlimited demand for training and why companies prefer to hire employees who are already educated (no cost of investment). The theory also explains why specific skills training related to a particular employer have more value than generalized training has for an employer, and vice versa for an employee.

It has been established in the literature that traditional input metrics such as training hours per employee, or training cost per employee, do not produce accurate predictions of organizational results. It has also been established that categories such as Leadership Practice, Employee Engagement, Knowledge Accessibility, Workforce Optimization and Learning Capacity be evaluated to determine organizational results of training initiatives. These categories could be either directly or indirectly related to an organizations training initiative, but would produce subjective results at best.

5.9 Specific versus General Training

General training constitutes more of the corporate training market than specific training. General training is also more valuable to employees because it will hold value in any organization they work for. Also, employee relations, managerial, and supervisory training constitutes the largest amount of general corporate training.

Specific skill training is less valuable to employees as it is non-transferrable to other organizations, or possibly even other positions within an organization. This may lead to it being more difficult to get employees engaged in specific skills training if they do not see it as being as valuable to them as general training options that may be available.

5.10 Training and Employee Satisfaction

The literature shows that corporate training is related to employee satisfaction and that this can be demonstrated by lower employee turnover and generally increased satisfaction. This result also relates to the idea that employees who have a higher set of skills due to corporate training are more satisfied with their employment. This also relates to the idea that this satisfaction from corporate training represents a significant source of competitive advantage for firms.

The other idea expressed in the literature relates to how employee satisfaction is related to training through alignment with how the training is structured, as well as to how goals and outcomes of the training are consistent with expectations.

In summary, training goals and objectives, inputs and outputs, expectations and structure of all parties involved in the training initiative must be aligned. These things are related to the degree of satisfaction that employees and the employer will experience as a result of the training initiative.

5.11 How Corporate Training Should Be Designed

The reality of corporate training is that employees will all learn in different ways, and learn different things as a result of a training initiative. Corporate training structures should be approached in this way. Employees, employers and training providers should be aware of a comprehensive approach to learning styles. Stakeholders should also note that the larger the group size, the less impact that instructional events have on individual learners.

It is also of note that many studies conducted indicate that there is no difference in the level of learning that takes place in an online environment. This is provided that different learning styles and multidimensional learning opportunities are considered.

Another idea within the corporate training design is to evaluate the structure and delivery based on the extent of goals and objectives met. This would include before and after training results, indirect benefits, and various performance metrics such as cost effectiveness, long term impacts, and other comparisons. It should be noted, however, that many of these evaluation metrics presented may produce more of a subjective result than an objective or accurate one.

5.12 Related Theories to Support Employee Training

Within the literature, various works often cited foundational works and theories that address corporate training in various contexts. In addition to foundational theories there are also contemporary works that describe the current global environment for businesses.

In summary, foundational works address human beings within the context of a working environment. Corporate training has a positive effect on human behavior in the workplace as it helps to address certain needs and things associated with positive or ideal employee behavior in workplaces.

Contemporary works focus on human beings as employees and organizations trying to adapt and cope with the current globalized environment that includes increasingly diverse populations and rapid technological advancement. Corporate training helps organizations and people to harness opportunities and mitigate risks that are associated with these factors.

5.13 Training for Small and Medium Sized Businesses

The research indicates that SMEs are not the majority of organizations that participate in corporate training for their employees. The largest users of corporate training are public organizations and large companies. This is cited as being due to a lack of time, space, staffing and financial resources. Technology is cited as a factor that could help SMEs leverage training opportunities.

In the United States and Canada most businesses fall within the definition of a small or medium sized business as defined by this report.

SME failure rates are high, and have been consistently high for years, with the majority failing within five years of being formed. Reasons for these failure rates are cited as being related to poor management. As many management techniques can be learned or developed, this would indicate that these owners or employees did not have time or resources to acquire or develop them before their business failed. This is one of the key challenges and opportunities that face SMEs.

There appears to be a consistent theme occurring in the literature that indicates that training produces long term benefits for organizations. The challenge is that often SMEs cannot afford to make the investment. This produces an interesting paradox where SMEs must plan for growth and investment in human resources and human capital, and still tend to day to day operations of the business.

A contrasting idea that appears in the literature is that it appears that large and public organizations train more employees. However, in the study cited in this report, in 2011 SMEs spent more money per employee than larger organizations. This indicates economies of scale as being another barrier for SMEs to engage in corporate training.

5.14 Corporate Training in Canada

Literature related to corporate training in Canada illustrates that SMEs in Canada face many of the same micro and macro environmental issues as their North American counterparts in the United States.

As the Canadian economy shifts towards a service based economy rather than a goods producing economy, intellectual capital becomes a differentiator in terms of Canadian businesses having a competitive advantage in the marketplace.

Demographic changes such as an aging population that is resulting in retirements, indicates the possibility of a shortage of skilled labor in the future.

As per the survey cited in this report, as of 2005 Ontario, British Columbia, Alberta, Saskatchewan, and Manitoba, have the majority (over 50%) of firms offering some type of corporate training. In Quebec and the Atlantic Provinces, less than 50% of firms located in these jurisdictions offer some type of training option for employees.

6.0 Analysis

From the major themes that appeared in the research literature, an analysis will now be done within the context of how those major themes relate to opportunities and challenges faced by small and medium sized businesses. Specifically, the analysis will address private sector businesses in Alberta in terms of investment in third party corporate training.

Limitations of this analysis are that most of the research and literature surrounding corporate training is broad in scale and scope. Much of the research was based on data collected in the United States and lacks an objective and directly relevant comparison of what is occurring for SMEs in Alberta. This relates to the additional limitation that there lacks specific data related to corporate training initiatives for Alberta, regardless of company size.

Data that is relevant for analysis of the literature as it relates to small and medium sized private sector businesses in Alberta was researched and is as follows:

- As of May 2013 the labor force in Alberta included 2.3 million people, with the largest portion of that (approx 15.7% or 361,000 people) included in the Edmonton, Red Deer, and Calgary regions (Alberta Education and Advanced Education, 2013).
- The service producing sector constitutes the majority of the workforce at 1.5 million people, with 0.6 million working in the goods producing sector in Alberta (Alberta Education and Advanced Education, 2013).
- Factors likely to affect Alberta's labor market in the future include: debt, deficits, and the pace of economic growth in the US, increasing oil and natural gas production, economic growth in emerging markets, interest rates, retirement of baby

boomers, interprovincial and international net migration
(Alberta Education and Advanced Education, 2013).

- From 2013 to 2016 the number of employed Albertans is
  expected to increase by 208,000 (Alberta Education and
  Advanced Education, 2013).
- Population is on an increasing trend, with 1.5% growth in
  2011, 2.5% in 2012, and 3.0% in 2013 with a current
  population of 3.9 million as of May 31, 2013 (Alberta
  Treasury Board and Finance, 2013).
- The number of third party corporate training firms as defined
  by the NAICS code 61143 in Alberta was 164 as of 2010
  (Industry Canada, 2013). This included businesses with a
  minimum income of $30,000.
- In 2011 Alberta has the lowest rate of employee absences in
  Canada (Statistics Canada as cited in University of Alberta,
  2013).
- There are a total of 152,543 businesses in Alberta. Small and
  medium sized business (5-499 employees) account for 40.8%
  (62,237) of the business in Alberta, with 59% (90,000) having
  1-4 employees, and 0.2 (306) having more than 500
  employees. (Industry Canada, 2013).

6.1 Opportunities

As indicated, in Alberta the service producing sectors constitute the
majority of employment in the province. As the literature states, as
businesses move towards a service based economy, knowledge and
skills become more important as a source of competitive advantage for
a firm. In this case third party training for SMEs can create a source of
competitive advantage.

Corporate training would allow an organization to better align its
organizational vision with that of its employees, and to put this vision
into implementation. Training that is aligned with corporate and

individual employee goals and objectives, has a greater chance of producing increased benefits for both individuals and organizations.

Organizations have an opportunity to determine their need for corporate training as dependent on their exposure and the potential impact of external environmental factors. Without doing this type of a needs analysis and continuous monitoring of the external environment, the organization could be negatively impacted by things like technological advancement or increased globalization (including outsourcing). These factors could be reduced through a corporate training initiative. Also, SMEs are unlikely to be spread across multiple jurisdictions and product mixes. Because of this a comprehensive needs assessment of corporate training to match external environment and organizational goals would likely have a long standing relevance to the entire organization, or at least the majority of it.

Overall, lower skilled workers receive less corporate training than employees with a higher level of skills and education. However, Alberta's labor market demographics continue to experience an aging workforce, increased population growth in the province, and an overall projected increase in the number of employed Albertans in the future. This combined with the fact that the majority of Albertans work in the service sector, with the ratio being 2.5 service sector workers for every 1 worker employed in the goods producing sector, leads to the fact that opportunities for lower skilled workers will likely increase. Training has also been shown to increase employee satisfaction and retention. The current economic, demographic, and labor market situation in Alberta provides SMEs with the opportunity to begin training initiatives for lower skilled workers. This will allow organizations to retain these workers, with their increased skill set acquired through training, to maintain a competitive advantage.

Corporate training initiatives also provide an organization's leadership with an opportunity to support organizational objectives through this vehicle. It has been demonstrated in this report that training success depends on the support of senior leadership within the organization.

Also related to this is that senior leadership ensures goal alignment and that the training is applicable in a practical way for employees to implement in their day to day work. A corporate training initiative would allow an organization to do all three of these things and receive the related benefits.

Technological advances provide SMEs with the opportunity to engage in corporate training by leveraging economies of scale. As well there are benefits from convenience, and the low cost of various types of third party training initiatives that are facilitated through an online platform. These innovations continue, and with increasing bandwidth for businesses in Alberta these options now typically include video conferencing and the ability to share video content and large files of material. As access increases and develops into the mobile platform, it is likely that more and more options available to SMEs will appear that will assist them in facilitating a corporate training initiative.

Employee satisfaction, as detailed in this report, leads to more productive workers, higher quality outputs, and is a significant source of competitive advantage. Corporate training provides SMEs with an opportunity to increase employee satisfaction, as the opportunity to participate in training has been shown to increase both employee skill sets and employee satisfaction. Again this relates back to having alignment of goals and objectives, and the degree to which this exists is directly related to the level of increased skills, productivity, and satisfaction experienced by the employee, thereby providing benefit to the employer.

As described in this report, there are several foundational theories that have existed and been heavily cited in several works that shows that corporate training has a positive effect on employee behavior in the workplace. This indicates that for those SMEs that do not engage in any type of training initiative, that there are opportunities to do so and will provide benefit to the organization. Additional supporting theories indicate that corporate training will help to mitigate factors associated with changes to an organization's external environment. Again, corporate training provides these benefits to SMEs as well as large and public organizations.

6.2 Challenges

The idea that lower skilled workers receive less training is reinforced by the Alberta data. The data shows that by industry, far more employees are employed in industries that do not traditionally spend a lot of resources on employee training. This poses the challenge of how these industries, or for that matter the majority of workers in Alberta, propose to mitigate or manage the macro environmental factors that will result in a lower competitive advantage for these industries and the employees in them.

The idea that from a longitudinal approach, that training can be evaluated to show quantifiable benefits to training, poses challenges to SMEs. Challenges exist because these evaluations would be costly, time consuming, and would always contain at least some degree of subjectivity related to the cause and effect of organizational outcomes. These outcomes would be related to the investment in third party corporate training. Based on the research, there would likely be no feasible way for an SME to evaluate its training in this way. Also from the 2011 survey data, SMEs are already spending more on the training itself than large organizations on a per employee basis. For an organization to invest further resources in an evaluation process would likely not be cost effective.

Benchmarking training initiatives for SMEs would be a challenge in Alberta due to the unique nature of the Alberta economy and the range of SMEs in the province. For an SME in Alberta to find a similar business in a similar industry to benchmark against may be unlikely.

The idea that organizational vision, leadership support, and training initiatives need to be in alignment to realize benefits from employee training poses challenges for SMEs. As indicated in this report, SMEs

49

have limited resources and it is likely that an organization that does not have time and financial resources to engage in corporate training, would also not have the resources to engage in a formal mission, vision, and value statement development initiative within the organization. Without goals and objectives that can be aligned to a corporate vision, organizational training is less likely to have a positive impact and generate beneficial returns for either the employee or the employer.

Training is always a shared investment, however, who pays the costs and who receives the benefits can vary to a large degree. There is also a large degree of subjectivity in terms of the exact value or benefit of a training initiative for either the employer or the employee. This is because many benefits of corporate training are intangible, and difficult to measure.

The idea around investment in human capital and human capital theory presents a challenge for SMEs as it can be difficult to articulate what exactly a training investment constitutes, and what the benefits are. Also because this theory states that increased productivity can only be had for a cost, what cost and how much productivity (or other training objectives) makes training worthwhile is also difficult to identify. Again this comes back to the difficulty of evaluating these factors and time, money, and the cost of other resources for SMEs.

The balance between specific and general training also creates challenges for SMEs. General training dominates the training marketplace; however this is also mostly being utilized by large and public organizations. These organizations may have more of a use, or more resources to utilize general training. SMEs may be more inclined towards skill specific training, as it holds more value for the organization as it cannot as easily be transferred elsewhere as can be done with general training. However, it is general training, specifically employee relations, management and supervisory training that dominates the marketplace. Again, SMEs would not have as many managers and supervisors as a large or public organization and may not have as prevalent a need for this type of training. It may also depend on the growth or decline of human resources in the organization, and what type of industry, to determine to what extent an organization engages in more general versus specific training. Amongst employees, general training is preferred, as it holds more value for them and can be transferred to other organizations or positions throughout their career. This might create limited interest or engagement in skills specific training, which is typically more beneficial for the organization.

The structure of the training itself poses challenges for SMEs. Because most SMEs will require their training design and facilitation to be done by a third party, this takes some of the control away from them in terms of what is included and how that material is delivered to employees. Training needs to be designed such that it aligns with stakeholder objectives, but that it also provides for the flexibility of individual learning needs. As detailed in this report, although the training may be designed for a group of employees, it is the individuals themselves that do the learning and each does so in a variety of different ways.

Employees of SMEs are not the majority of employees that engage in corporate training, those employees are in both large and public sector organizations. This presumably would indicate that the majority of training providers are catering towards the large corporation and public organization target market. This presents a challenge for SMEs looking for products and services that will adequately serve their needs in terms of structure, design, and pricing.

SME failure rates have been historically high and continue to be so. Reasons often cited are that organizations lacked the skills to compete in the marketplace that could potentially have been acquired through a corporate training initiative. This creates challenges because organizations need resources to invest in training, which they may not be able to acquire, until they get the skills to do so. This is compounded by the data cited in this report from a 2011 study indicating that per employee, SMEs spend more on average than large

51

and public organizations. This poses the challenge of training in terms of economies of scale and the kinds of efficiencies that it provides.

In Alberta, 57% of businesses offer some type of corporate training. However this means that 43% do not. With the level of positive benefits that corporate training provides, and the potential risks mitigated by it, the challenges to implementing corporate training in the 43% of Alberta businesses needs to be addressed. The reasons for this are that it will be for the betterment of those organizations, their employees, the Alberta economy, and society in general.

7.0 Recommendations

The following recommendations will address management issues and provide practical application of the research and analysis contained in this report. This will allow organizations to leverage opportunities and overcome challenges for small and medium sized private sector businesses with regards to investing in a corporate training initiative.

7.1 Recommendations for SMEs

When not to Invest in Corporate Training

It is recommended that any organization that does not have clearly defined goals and objectives for their business, should not engage in a formal corporate training initiative. These goals and objectives are in terms of a vision and/or mission statement, target objectives, or similar factors that can be quantified and qualified as goals. The reason for this is because, as indicated in this report, the degree to which corporate training is successful depends upon the degree of alignment with organizational goals.

A secondary recommendation in this area would be to also have an awareness of employee goals which ideally would be in alignment with organizational goals. If it cannot be determined that employee goals are in alignment with organizational goals, this should first be accomplished before the organization looks at making an investment in corporate training.

Which Companies Should Invest In Corporate Training

It is recommended that all SME's in Alberta, particularly those in service producing sectors, develop a formal corporate training initiative for its employees in order to leverage the shift towards a knowledge based economy. It will also help to ensure that employees continue to

53

have the skills to remain a source of competitive advantage for the organization.

Corporate training has also been shown to have a positive impact related to various human behavioral theories in terms of people in the workplace. Any corporation that is heavily reliant on its workforce (which would presumably be most or all) would be able to leverage this fact by engaging in a corporate training initiative.

What Should Be In Place Before Investing In Corporate Training

It is recommended that any organization looking to undergo a corporate training initiative first conduct a needs assessment either independently or with the assistance of a training provider.

The needs assessment may proceed as follows:

- In order to leverage employee satisfaction related to corporate training, it is recommended that an organizations senior leadership solicit input from employees and managers with regard to their goals and objectives within the organization.
- From there it is important to structure a training initiative with a third party corporate trainer that aligns these components.

As described in this report, the extent to which these factors are in alignment determines the degree of success (as defined by stakeholder goals and objectives).

How Much and What Type of Resources to Invest

It is recommended that SMEs engage third party corporate training providers to assess and deliver training needs of the organization, for both general and skills specific training.

The reason for this recommendation is that for most SMEs, resources such as money, space, time, and staffing requirements for

54

implementing a corporate training initiative may be limited and may need to go to more immediate short term priorities.

A third party training provider will allow SMEs to leverage economies of scale. It will also allow for SMEs to take advantage of low cost options from these providers to create increased value for organizations that may not be able to do this type of training with their own facilities and resources. This would be true for either general or skills specific training, depending on the needs of the organization as defined by their goals and objectives.

Who Should Receive Corporate Training

It is important that any training initiative be approached as a mutual investment for both the employee and employer. Because it has been shown that it is factors that are within the employer's control that drive success in training initiatives, it is recommended that it is the employer then who should initiate who receives what corporate training in the organization.

To address the challenges that are created by training being a shared benefit, it is recommended that all benefits and costs for both the employee and employer be identified. In this way, an agreement can be made that meets the needs of both parties where benefits can be shared according to the goals, costs, and benefits of each party. This may include sharing the financial cost of the training, a time period where the employee would need to pay back any employer subsidized fees towards the training, allowing the training to occur on work time, etc.

It is also recommended that opportunities for training be equally distributed in the organization. Traditionally, lower skilled workers or employees with lower levels of education are not provided as many opportunities for training as higher skilled or more highly educated employees. With the current economic environment in Alberta, the results of corporate training on increased retention and employee satisfaction indicate that training all employees may result in benefits for both the employee and the organization.

How To Evaluate Success

It is recommended that evaluation of training initiatives by SMEs to determine a return on the investment not be conducted. Any kind of an evaluation would be costly, and largely subjective, and for an SME would likely reduce the cost effectiveness of the training initiative. Instead, to address this challenge of evaluation, it is recommended that organizations ensure that training is aligned with organizational goals and that training is applicable and functional in meeting the needs of the organization. In this way, it has been shown that longitudinal studies indicate that training does provide benefit. However, there may also be indirect factors affecting results. It would be reasonable to assume that as long as training is aligned with organizational and employee objectives, that over the long term training will generate benefits for all stakeholders.

To mitigate the challenges associated with a variety of learning styles, it is recommended that any training initiative include a comprehensive complement of learning facilitation methods in order to allow for the accommodation of individual learning needs. Audio, visual, and interactive components will be important parts of the training initiative. In particular, any type of component that integrates a practical application of learning into an employee's day to day work environment will produce increased results compared to an initiative where these components are missing or lacking.

It is also recommended that any type of benchmarking used to evaluate training should only occur within the organization itself, due to the lack of data and comparable SMEs in Alberta. An additional caveat is to be aware of the large degree of subjectivity that would be inherent in relating employee training to any organizational outcome, as there would likely be many indirect factors that would have an influence on the outcome.

Ongoing Support

It is recommended that an organization's management and senior leadership continue to demonstrate ongoing support for organizational goals and objectives by linking them to a corporate training initiative.

It has been shown that the degree to which corporate training initiatives are successful is in direct proportion to the level of support exhibited by management and senior leadership of organizations.

8.0 Conclusion

For small and medium sized private sector enterprises (SMEs) in Alberta, this report shows that there is a need to realize opportunities and overcome challenge with regards to implementing an employee corporate training initiative for each of these businesses in the province.

The findings of this research are important because, as this report indicates, 43% of Alberta businesses do not offer any type of formal corporate training option for their employees.

The importance of corporate training is underlined by data included in this report indicating demographic changes, technological advances, increased globalization, and the potential for a shortage of skilled labor in Alberta in the future. The presence of these changing variables shows that there is a clear need for corporate training for all organizations.

Broader implications to consider are that SME failure rates continue to be high. Part of the reason, as cited in this report, is a lack of knowledge and understanding about how to manage the business. This could be resolved through training, however, this takes resources that are often allocated to more immediate competing priorities.

Also, there is the cost / benefit idea behind an organization being hesitant to invest in an employee by training them with the possibility they might leave the organization. This often creates a self-fulfilling prophesy of an employee leaving an organization for one that does offer this type of investment in employees.

8.1 Key Findings and Recommendations

Application of the research has been ranked and summarized in a Key Findings and Recommendations Matrix (See Appendix A).

These findings were ranked 1 (low) to 5 (high) in terms of how important each factor was to the success of each particular focus area. Based on these rankings the conclusions for each focus area are listed below:

Benefits of Corporate Training

Determining a return on investment (ROI), ranks low, on the list of factors impacting the success of an organization receiving the benefits of third party corporate training. Training that supports organizational goals is the most important factor, followed by training that aligns with employee goals. Although it is likely true that a skilled workforce will benefit society as a whole, this aspect may be of lower priority to an organization attempting to benefit from a training initiative.

It is recommended that organizations, specifically SMEs, take a holistic approach to third party corporate training and its benefits.

The Need for Corporate Training

Training is needed for all businesses in the increasingly developing knowledge economy. Certain groups, particularly small and medium sized private business, are not represented well as organizations that provide training to their employees.

It is recommended that in order to attract, retain, and remain competitive from a human resources standpoint, that SMEs address the need to employ third party training in their organizations.

Evaluating Training Initiatives

For SMEs the ability to evaluate all of the possible impacts that training may have on operations ranks low as a factor that will impact the success of this type of an evaluation.

It is recommended that SMEs focus the evaluation of their training in terms of how well training aligns with organizational and employee goals.

Training as a Shared Investment

Sharing cost, benefits, risks, and rewards between the organization and its employees is a mid-range factor in terms of how this impacts the success of a training initiative. The options are almost unlimited in terms of how the costs, benefits, risks, and rewards could be shared. However, it is this sharing of these factors which enhances the employer employee relationship, which ranks at the highest level in terms of success of implementing corporate training.

It is recommended that organizations and employee find ways to share the investment of training that aligns with the goals and objectives of each stakeholder in the most amicable way. In this way, approaching training as a shared investment will enhance the employer employee relationship which will increase the value and success of the training.

Employee Groups Participating in Corporate Training

As a whole, it is recognized that employees with a low skill set and lower levels of education receive less opportunities for corporate training than those individuals at the other end of the spectrum. This is an important factor for employers and employees to consider, in that lower skilled workers may benefit just as much or more from similar opportunities.

It is recommended that organizations take the initiative to define a structure for their corporate training that gives access to all levels of employees that need the training. For industries that typically do not engage in any form of corporate training, it is recommended that they start, based on the benefits cited in this report. If organizations are finding difficulty doing this on their own, it is recommended they seek the assistance of a third party corporate trainer to help define this structure.

Keys to Successful Corporate Training

Alignment of organizational and employee goals is one of the most important components to a successful corporate training initiative. A secondary component that lends itself to the level of practicality of the training is the ability to link the training, or components of the training, to actual organizational operations. Linking a practical component is a mid-range factor for training success. Although it enhances the learning experience, if it is not possible due to logistics or resource scarcity, training should not be foregone simply because this component cannot be integrated.

It is recommended that organizations work with a third party training provider to integrate practical components of their operations into any training initiatives.

Online Corporate Training

Online options are becoming more and more important for organizations to have success in their training initiatives. Economies of scale, low cost, and convenience are a few benefits, in addition to the fact that it has been shown that online learning meets, and in some cases exceeds, the individual needs of learners.

It is recommended that organizations assess their required level of online learning integration with their training initiatives. This is due to the fact that online training can have various cost structures, and various levels of financial and other investments in resources and infrastructure.

Human Capital Theory

Awareness of human capital theory and how it is related to corporate training is very important to its success. The ability for an organization to invest and increase the value of its human resources is one of the key drivers of corporate training demand.

Because training has marginal costs and benefits, it is recommended that organizations look closely at their training options to determine how much training and what type of training they want to invest in. As stated in this report, the alignment of organizational and employee goals will result in increased human capital, and organizations will want to choose training options with this in mind.

Specific versus General Training

In general, specific training provides more marginal value for the organization than general training, provided the employee stays with the organization. General training provides more marginal value for the employee as it is transferrable to other positions and organizations.

It is a high ranking factor for training success that organizations consider the appropriate mix of skills specific versus general training. This can, and likely should, be done without the assistance of a third party training provider as they are unlikely to know the operational needs of a particular business.

It is recommended that organizations consider the alignment of organizational and employee goals as related to the findings in this report when creating this training mix. Employees are more willing to participate in training that is of value to them and organizations will want to offer operationally beneficial training. Meeting both stakeholder needs amicably will be a key component to a successful training initiative.

Training and Employee Satisfaction

Training opportunities have been shown to increase employee satisfaction and decrease turnover rates.

It is recommended that although research has shown this to be the case, it is an important consideration for training that organizations refrain from tracking these statistics. As with other evaluations of training cited in this report, this type of analysis will likely result in subjective or incorrect conclusions as there are a variety of factors that will impact these metrics.

How Corporate Training Should be Designed

Training design is a highly rated factor for the success of a training initiative. The structure needs to meet the needs of various learning styles, as well as ensure that organizational and learner needs are aligned.

It is recommended that organizations utilize the experience of professional third party corporate trainers in order to utilize an already developed program tailored to an organization's needs or to develop something from the ground up.

Related Theories to Support Employee Training

As shown in this report, in general, employee training provides a positive effect on human behavior both personally and professionally for learners.

It is recommended that organizations seek out guidance from third party corporate trainers in order to develop communication plans for their employees to gain a higher degree of buy-in for any training initiative.

Training in the Context of Small and Medium Sized Businesses

SME failure rates have been shown in this report to be historically high. Many reasons cited are that owners or executives lack the necessary management knowledge and experience to make the venture successful. This could be mitigated by investing in training. This is a highly rated factor for both the success of training and the organization itself.

It is noted that a shortage or resources often contributes to the lack of training opportunities prevalent at SMEs. This creates a case of cause and effect whereby more training may have saved the business, but the business had no money to invest in training.

It is therefore recommended that SMEs come up with a comprehensive plan, based on the research and recommendations contained in this report, to integrate corporate training into their business plan.

Corporate Training in Canada

The globalized economy and a shift towards service based economies, in addition to demographic changes and technological advancements, are becoming increasing factors impacting organizations. It is recommended that organizations become cognizant of how corporate training can enhance their ability to adapt to changes, and mitigate risks resulting from these factors.

In Summary

This report indicates that small and medium sized business can feasibly embark on a third party corporate training initiative that will benefit their organization and allow the business to remain competitive in an ever-changing marketplace.

There is a cost to this training, but the true cost is to ignore the need to invest in the human resources of a business. As it relates to employee satisfaction, higher quality outputs, lower turnover, increased diversity and change management, as well as a vehicle for aligning organizational values and vision, third party corporate training benefits provide substantial returns for the cost.

References

Alberta Enterprise and Advanced Education. (2013). 2013 Monthly

Labour Force Statistics. Retrieved from

http://eae.alberta.ca/labour-and-immigration/labour-market-

information/labour-force-statistics-and-annual-reviews/2013-

monthly-labour-force-statistics.aspx

Alberta Treasury Board and Finance. (2013, May 30). About Alberta's

Economy and Demography. Retrieved from

http://www.finance.alberta.ca/aboutalberta/

Amélie Bernier, & Cousineau, J. (2010). The impact of training on

productivity in canadian firms: Estimating distributed lags from

the WES 1999-2005. *International Journal of Interdisciplinary*

Social Sciences, 5(7), 231-239. Retrieved from http://0-

search.ebscohost.com.aupac.lib.athabascau.ca/login.aspx?direct=t

rue&AuthType=url,ip,uid&db=a9h&AN=66384551&site=ehost-

live

Appendix A: Corporate professional development and training. (2002).

ASHE-ERIC Higher Education Report, 29(1), 87. Retrieved from

http://0-

search.ebscohost.com.aupac.lib.athabascau.ca/login.aspx?direct=t

rue&AuthType=url,ip,uid&db=a9h&AN=10296954&site=ehost-

live

Ballot, G., Fakhfakh, F., & Taymaz, E. (2006). Who benefits from

training and R&D, the firm or the workers? *British Journal of*

Industrial Relations, 44(3), 473-495. doi: 10.1111/j.1467-

8543.2006.00509.x

Bassi, L., & McMurrer, D. (2007). Maximizing your return on people.

Harvard Business Review, 85(3), 115-123. Retrieved from

http://0-

search.ebscohost.com.aupac.lib.athabascau.ca/login.aspx?direct=t

rue&AuthType=url,ip,uid&db=bth&AN=23927003&site=ehost-

live

Batool, A., & Batool, B. (2012). Effects of employees training on the
organizational competitive advantage: Empirical study of private
sector of islamabad, pakistan. *Far East Journal of Psychology &
Business, 6*(1), 59-72. Retrieved from http://0-
search.ebscohost.com.aupac.lib.athabascau.ca/login.aspx?direct=t
rue&AuthType=url,ip,uid&db=a9h&AN=75235780&site=ehost-
live

Becker, G. S. (1964). Human Capital – A Theoretical and Empirical
Analysis, with Special Reference to Education. Columbia
University Press: New York and London

Bird, M. M. (1973). Training wanted for corporate level management
of small manufacturing firms. *Training & Development Journal,
27*(9), 40. Retrieved from http://0-
search.ebscohost.com.aupac.lib.athabascau.ca/login.aspx?direct=t
rue&AuthType=url,ip,uid&db=a9h&AN=7469519&site=ehost-
live

Cekada, T. L. (2011). Need training? *Professional Safety, 56*(12), 28-

34. Retrieved from http://0-

search.ebscohost.com.aupac.lib.athabascau.ca/login.aspx?direct=t

rue&AuthType=url,ip,uid&db=a9h&AN=67633067&site=ehost-

live

Chan, P., Miller, R., & Monroe, E. (2009). Cognitive apprenticeship as

an instructional strategy for solving corporate training challenges.

TechTrends: Linking Research & Practice to Improve Learning,

53(6), 35-41. doi: 10.1007/s11528-009-0341-3

Cohen, S. (1998). Big ideas for trainers in small companies. *Training &*

Development, 52(4), 26. Retrieved from http://0-

search.ebscohost.com.aupac.lib.athabascau.ca/login.aspx?direct=t

rue&AuthType=url,ip,uid&db=a9h&AN=502197&site=ehost-

live

Craig, L. R. (1996). The ASTD Training and Development Handbook.

McGraw Hill: New York

Crist, T., Presley, L., & Zenger, J. (1992). Partnerships net big wins. *Training & Development, 46*(9), 38. Retrieved from http://0-search.ebscohost.com.aupac.lib.athabascau.ca/login.aspx?direct=true&AuthType=url,ip,uid&db=a9h&AN=9805872&site=ehost-live

Dobrovolny, J. (2006). How adults learn from Self- Paced, Technology Based corporate training: New focus for learners, new focus for designers. *Distance Education, 27*(2), 155-170. doi: 10.1080/01587910600789506

Gagne, M. R., Briggs, J.L. (1979). Principles of Instructional Design. Library of Congress: United States of America

Hansson, B. (2008). *Job-related training and benefits for individuals: A review of evidence and explanations.* Unpublished manuscript.from http://search.proquest.com/docview/189839928?accountid=8408

Hardman, W., & Robertson, L. (2012). What motivates employees to persist with online training? one canadian workplace study. *International Journal of Business, Humanities & Technology,* *2*(5), 66-78. Retrieved from http://0-search.ebscohost.com.aupac.lib.athabascau.ca/login.aspx?direct=true&AuthType=url,ip,uid&db=a9h&AN=83410863&site=ehost-live

Harris, P. (2005). Small businesses bask in training's spotlight. *T+d,* *59*(2), 46-50. Retrieved from http://0-search.ebscohost.com.aupac.lib.athabascau.ca/login.aspx?direct=true&AuthType=url,ip,uid&db=a9h&AN=15987423&site=ehost-live

Industry Canada. (2013, Feb 14). SME Benchmarking Tool. Retrieved from http://www.ic.gc.ca/eic/site/pp-pp.nsf/eng/home

Industry Canada. (2012, August 3). Key Small Business Statistics – July 2012. Retrieved from http://www.ic.gc.ca/eic/site/061.nsf/eng/02714.html

Joo, Y. J., Kyu, Y. L., & Kim, S. M. (2012). A model for predicting

learning flow and achievement in corporate e-learning. *Journal of*

Educational Technology & Society, 15(1), 313-325. Retrieved

from http://0-

search.ebscohost.com.aupac.lib.athabascau.ca/login.aspx?direct=t

rue&AuthType=url,ip,uid&db=a9h&AN=72954742&site=ehost-

live

Kelly, L. (1984). Small business's big training needs. *Training &*

Development Journal, 38(6), 36. Retrieved from http://0-

search.ebscohost.com.aupac.lib.athabascau.ca/login.aspx?direct=t

rue&AuthType=url,ip,uid&db=a9h&AN=9075521&site=ehost-

live

Kirkpatrick, J., & Kirkpatrick, W. K. (2010). Training on trial. *Journal*

for Quality & Participation, 33(3), 26-31. Retrieved from

http://0-

search.ebscohost.com.aupac.lib.athabascau.ca/login.aspx?direct=t

rue&AuthType=url,ip,uid&db=a9h&AN=55192647&site=ehost-

live

73

Kyndt, E., Dochy, F., Onghena, P., & Baert, H. (2013). The learning

intentions of low-qualified employees: A multilevel approach.

Adult Education Quarterly, 63(2), 165-189. doi:

10.1177/0741713612454324

Matalonga, S., & Feliu, T. S. (2012). Calculating return on investment

of training using process variation. *IET Software, 6*(2), 140-147.

doi: 10.1049/iet-sen.2011.0024

McEvoy, G. M., & Buller, P. F. (1990). Five uneasy pieces in the

training evaluation puzzle. *Training & Development Journal,*

44(8), 39. Retrieved from http://0-

search.ebscohost.com.aupac.lib.athabascau.ca/login.aspx?direct=t

rue&AuthType=url,ip,uid&db=a9h&AN=9089544&site=ehost-

live

Melnik, M. S. (2008). The rational, emotional & physical approach to

training. *Professional Safety, 53*(1), 49-51. Retrieved from

http://0-

search.ebscohost.com.aupac.lib.athabascau.ca/login.aspx?direct=t

rue&AuthType=url,ip,uid&db=a9h&AN=28096552&site=ehost-

live

Meyer, S. R., & Marsick, V. J. (2003). Professional development in

corporate training. *New Directions for Adult & Continuing*

Education, (98), 75. Retrieved from http://0-

search.ebscohost.com.aupac.lib.athabascau.ca/login.aspx?direct=t

rue&AuthType=url,ip,uid&db=a9h&AN=9973777&site=ehost-

live

Miller, L. (2012). 2012 ASTD state of the industry report:

Organizations continue to invest in workplace learning. *T+d,*

66(11), 42-48. Retrieved from http://0-

search.ebscohost.com.aupac.lib.athabascau.ca/login.aspx?direct=t

rue&AuthType=url,ip,uid&db=a9h&AN=82939631&site=ehost-

live

Newton, R., & Doonga, N. (2007). Corporate e-learning: Justification

for implementation and evaluation of benefits. A study examining

the views of training managers and training providers. *Education*

for Information, 25(2), 111-130. Retrieved from http://0-

search.ebscohost.com.aupac.lib.athabascau.ca/login.aspx?direct=t

rue&AuthType=url,ip,uid&db=a9h&AN=25797968&site=ehost-

live

Newton, R., & Doonga, N. (2007). Corporate e-learning: Justification

for implementation and evaluation of benefits. A study examining

the views of training managers and training providers. *Education*

for Information, 25(2), 111-130. Retrieved from http://0-

search.ebscohost.com.aupac.lib.athabascau.ca/login.aspx?direct=t

rue&AuthType=url,ip,uid&db=a9h&AN=25797968&site=ehost-

live

Plate, J. – Statistics Canada (2005). The Education Services Industry in

Canada. Retrieved from

http://publications.gc.ca/Collection/Statcan/81-595-MIE/81-

595-MIE2005033.pdf

Rivera, R. J. (2010). *What is a pound of training worth? A longitudinal study of the effects of training investments on financial performance in firms.* (Ph.D., Stanford University). *ProQuest Dissertations and Theses,* Retrieved from http://search.proquest.com/docview/305224058?accountid=8408. (305224058).

Rossett, A. (2002). The ASTD E-Learning Handbook. McGraw Hill: New York

Salas-Velasco, M. (2007). Graduates on the labor market: Formal and informal post-school training investments. *Higher Education, 54*(2), 227-246. doi: 10.1007/s10734-005-3092-x

Statistics Canada. (2013, May 10). Labour force characteristics, seasonally adjusted, by province (monthly). Retrieved from http://www.statcan.gc.ca/tables-tableaux/sum-som/l01/cst01/lfss01c-eng.htm

Statistics Canada. (2010, March 17). North American Industry
Classification (NAICS)

2007. Retrieved from

http://stds.statcan.gc.ca/naics-scian/2007/cs-rc-
eng.asp?criteria=61143

Statistics Canada (2000, February). Failure rates for new Canadian

firms: New perspective on entry and exit. Retrieved from

http://www.statcan.gc.ca/pub/61-526-x/61-526-x1999001-

eng.pdf

University of Alberta. (2012). Labour Force Statistics. Retrieved from

http://guides.library.ualberta.ca/content.php?pid=50949&sid=

377032

Appendix A – Key Findings and Recommendations Matrix

Focus Area	*Economic Benefits of Third Party Training*	*Ranking of Factors Related to Focus Area 1(low) - 5(high)*	*Training Options for SMEs*
Benefits of Corporate Training			
	Determining ROI of Training	1	A third party training provider may attempt to determine an ROI, as well as align training with organizational and employee goals. Alternatively, the organization could do this on their own, or a combination of the two options.
	Training Supports Organizational Goals	5	
	Training Supports Employee Goals	4	
	Training Benefits Society Overall	3	
The Need for Corporate Training			
	Training Needed to Compete in a Globalised, Knowledge Economy	5	Organizations can choose which employees receive training opportunities, and which do not. This can be done with the assistance of a third party training provider, or independently.

	Certain Employee Groups are Under Represented in Training	4	
	Training Can Help With Workforce Retention	5	
Evaluating Training Initiatives			
	Could potentially link quantitative and qualitative benefits to training initiatives	1	Organizations could rely on third party trainers to provide this information, look at the relevant research and data that already exists, or attempt to do this independently.
Training as a Shared Investment			
	Share costs and benefits with employees	3	Options for this could include a division of financial and reward risk sharing based on industry standards, past organizational practice, or something new. This could occur with or without the assistance of a third party training provider.
	Share risk and reward with employees	3	
	Enhances the employer employee relationship	5	

80

Third Party Corporate Training
Opportunities and Challenges Facing Small and Medium Sized
Businesses in Alberta

Employee Groups Participating in Corporate Training			
	Ability to provide training opportunities to lower skilled employee groups	4	An organization can decide on the structure of training opportunities with or without the assistance of a third party corporate trainer.
	Can enhance opportunities for employees with previous education	4	
Keys to Successful Corporate Training			
	Training and goal alignment will produce high quality results	5	Organizations will want to work towards training being offered that is aligned with organizational and employee goals. They may wish to do this with or without the assistance of a third party trainer.
	Ability to practically link components of training to operations	3	
Online Corporate Training			

	Leverage economies of scale to provide lower cost and more accessible training	4	An organization can decide to what degree it would like to integrate online corporate training into its training options. Online training can have various options and cost structures that have to be considered.
Human Capital Theory			
	The ability to invest in the human resources of the organization, increasing its value	5	Organizations will want to decide to what degree they want to invest in training as it relates to their human capital. Training has a cost which increases marginal value, the extent of which needs to be determined by the organization.
Specific Versus General Training			
	Specific training will provide more marginal value for the organization than general training, provided the employee stays with the organization	5	The mix of skills specific and general training will need to be determined by the organization. This can be done with or without the assistance of a third party training provider

Training and Employee Satisfaction			
	Training increases employee satisfaction and lowers turnover	5	Organizations will need to decide whether they will track these factors or not, and to what degree.
How Corporate Training Should Be Designed			
	Allows for the learning needs of all employees to be catered to	4	Organizations can use training that has been designed by a third party trainer, or work with one to develop a custom training structure.
	Allows for the structure of training to align with the organization and it's employee's needs	5	
Related Theories to Support Employee Training			
	Training provides a positive effect on human behavior	5	Organizations may choose how they wish to support the successes or needs of improvement for their training initiative.

Training in the Context of SMEs			
	Training has benefits and SMEs are underrepresented in terms of organizations that provide corporate training to their employees	5	SMEs can choose whether or not to engage in a third party corporate training initiative, and to what extent.
	SME failure rates are high, often cites for reasons of poor management	5	
Corporate Training in Canada			
	Canadian economy shifting towards a knowledge and service based economy	4	The Canadian economy presents numerous options for SMEs to engage in some form of corporate training to leverage benefits and mitigate the risks that come with the global, technological, and demographic shifts that are taking place in the market.
	Demographic changes means training can help to align employee and organizational goals	4	

Index

A

ability, 16, 18, 20, 22, 27,
   39, 48, 60-62, 64
Academic Search
   Complete, 33
accommodation, 56
accountability, 22
actualization, 25
adaptable, 8
adult education and
   training, 30
adults, 18
advantage, 21, 28, 41, 44,
   46-49, 54-55
Alberta, 7-65
Alberta Education and
   Advanced Education,
   45-46

Alberta Treasury Board
   and Finance, 46
Albertans, 46-47
alignment, 38-39, 41,
   48-49, 53-54, 61-62
American Society for
   Training and
   Development (ASTD),
   32
analysis, 7, 13, 32, 45, 47,
   53, 63
application, 17, 38, 53,
   56, 59
ASHE Higher Education
   Report, 11-17
Ashton, 16
assessment, 47, 54
assistance, 54, 61-62
Atlantic Provinces, 27,
   30, 44
attitudes, 22, 26
awareness, 21, 53, 62

B

C

D

E

economic benefits, 8
economic development, 19, 40
economies of scale, 16-17, 27, 29, 38-39, 43, 48, 52, 55, 61
Edmonton, 45
Education, 11, 15, 18-19, 22, 28-31, 34, 37-38, 45-47, 55, 60
educational services, 31
educational significance, 24
effectiveness, 8, 24, 42, 56
efficiencies, 52
elearning, 28
employee engagement, 20, 40
employee groups, 15, 35, 37, 60
employee productivity, 8
employee relations, 21, 40, 50
employee satisfaction, 21, 36, 41, 47-48, 54, 63-64
employee training, 8-11, 15-17, 21, 24, 27-28, 30, 35-37, 39-40, 42, 49, 56, 63
employee turnover, 21, 41

employer, 11-12, 14, 20-22, 31, 35-37, 40-41, 48, 50, 55, 60
employer financed training, 11
employer satisfaction, 21
employer sponsored training, 11, 21
employers, 13, 19, 27, 31, 41, 60
employment, 20, 31, 41, 46
enterprises, 7, 16, 27, 58
environmental, 20, 35, 44, 47, 49
esteem needs, 25
evaluation, 12-14, 23, 25, 36, 42, 49, 56, 60
evaluation methods, 13
evaluation of training, 12, 25, 56
evaluations, 13, 34, 49, 63
expectations, 41
expenditure, 29
experimental, 26
expired, 19
exponentially, 26
exposure, 47
extended support, 24

I

J

K

R

S

www.ingramcontent.com/pod-product-compliance
Lightning Source LLC
Chambersburg PA
CBHW060630210326
41520CB00010B/1541